# The Ultimate Brag Book About yourself

# The Ultimate Brag Book About yourself

A hundred questions about
how awesome you are!

MARLA J. ALBERTIE, M. ED.

The Ultimate Brag Book About Yourself: A hundred questions about how awesome you are

Author: Marla J. Albertie

contact@truthspeakscoaching.com truthspeaksgroup.com

Research: Marla J. Albertie
Cover by: Analisa Orquin

Published by: Truth Speaks Publishing a brand of Truth Speaks Group, LLC. Jacksonville, Florida

ISBN: 979-8-88759-292-3 (paperback)
ISBN: 979-8-88759-293-0 (ebook)

Do you want more tools for work/life harmony?
Sick of trying to "balance" everything in life?


Click on the link below to subscribe to my email list
and get your FREE work/life harmony workbook!


book.truthspeakscoaching.com

# Contents

# Introduction

Can you imagine all the things you like, love, and adore in one book?

All your favorites captured at one time with space to write more.

So, why did I write this book?

How often do we brag about ourselves, take time to think about what makes us happy, or do the things we like? If I had to guess, not as often as you would like.

This book has been on my heart for years and I am finally getting it out to the world. You deserve to brag about yourself, so why not?

Not only is this a bragging book, but it is a book of ideas you can use to start your next project, business, career move, or anything your heart desires.

So how does it work?

Each topic/list has a "number" to reach because the goal is to get you to stretch your thinking. Need more space? Don't worry, there are extra lines per number so you can add more and there are extra pages in the back of the book for you to create your own.

Ready to start bragging?

Have fun!

# My 5 favorite holidays...

1. _____
   _____
   _____
   _____

2. _____
   _____
   _____
   _____

3. _____
   _____
   _____
   _____

4. _____
   _____
   _____

5. _____
   _____
   _____
   _____

# Happiness defined in 5 words...

1. _____
   _____
   _____
   _____

2. _____
   _____
   _____
   _____

3. _____
   _____
   _____
   _____

4. _____
   _____
   _____
   _____

5. _____
   _____
   _____
   _____

*10 things that impress me...*

1. _____
   _____
   _____
   _____

2. _____
   _____
   _____
   _____

3. _____
   _____
   _____
   _____

4. _____
   _____
   _____
   _____

5. _____
   _____
   _____
   _____

6. _____
   _____
   _____
   _____

7. _____
   _____
   _____
   _____

Marla J. Albertie, M. Ed.

8. _____
   _____
   _____
   _____

9. _____
   _____
   _____
   _____

10. _____
   _____
   _____
   _____

# 10 cars I like...

1. _____
   _____
   _____
   _____

2. _____
   _____
   _____
   _____

3. _____
   _____
   _____
   _____

4. _____
   _____
   _____
   _____

5. _____
   _____
   _____
   _____

6. _____
   _____
   _____
   _____

7. _____
   _____
   _____
   _____

Marla J. Albertie, M. Ed.

8. _____
   _____
   _____
   _____

9. _____
   _____
   _____
   _____

10. _____
    _____
    _____
    _____

# 10 "me time" things I do for self-care...

1. _____
   _____
   _____
   _____

2. _____
   _____
   _____
   _____

3. _____
   _____
   _____
   _____

4. _____
   _____
   _____
   _____

5. _____
   _____
   _____

6. _____
   _____
   _____
   _____

7. _____
   _____
   _____
   _____

Marla J. Albertie, M. Ed.

8. _____
   _____
   _____
   _____

9. _____
   _____
   _____
   _____

10. _____
   _____
   _____
   _____

# 10 things I will have done in 5 years...

1. _____
   _____
   _____
   _____

2. _____
   _____
   _____
   _____

3. _____
   _____
   _____
   _____

4. _____
   _____
   _____
   _____

5. _____
   _____
   _____
   _____

6. _____
   _____
   _____
   _____

7. _____
   _____
   _____
   _____

Marla J. Albertie, M. Ed.

8. _____
   _____
   _____
   _____

9. _____
   _____
   _____
   _____

10. _____
    _____
    _____
    _____

## 10 things I will have done in 10 years...

1. _____
   _____
   _____
   _____

2. _____
   _____
   _____
   _____

3. _____
   _____
   _____
   _____

4. _____
   _____
   _____
   _____

5. _____
   _____
   _____
   _____

6. _____
   _____
   _____
   _____

7. _____
   _____
   _____
   _____

Marla J. Albertie, M. Ed.

8. _____
   _____
   _____
   _____

9. _____
   _____
   _____
   _____

10. _____
    _____
    _____
    _____

## 10 things I will have done in 20 years...

1. _____
   _____
   _____
   _____

2. _____
   _____
   _____
   _____

3. _____
   _____
   _____
   _____

4. _____
   _____
   _____
   _____

5. _____
   _____
   _____

6. _____
   _____
   _____

7. _____
   _____
   _____

Marla J. Albertie, M. Ed.

8. _____
   _____
   _____
   _____

9. _____
   _____
   _____
   _____

10. _____
    _____
    _____
    _____

## 10 things I will have done in 30 years...

1. _____
_____
_____
_____

2. _____
_____
_____
_____

3. _____
_____
_____
_____

4. _____
_____
_____
_____

5. _____
_____
_____
_____

6. _____
_____
_____
_____

7. _____
_____
_____
_____

Marla J. Albertie, M. Ed.

8. _____
   _____
   _____
   _____

9. _____
   _____
   _____
   _____

10. _____
   _____
   _____
   _____

# 10 things I love about myself...

1. _____
   _____
   _____
   _____

2. _____
   _____
   _____
   _____

3. _____
   _____
   _____
   _____

4. _____
   _____
   _____
   _____

5. _____
   _____
   _____
   _____

6. _____
   _____
   _____

7. _____
   _____
   _____

Marla J. Albertie, M. Ed.

8. _____
   _____
   _____
   _____

9. _____
   _____
   _____
   _____

10. _____
    _____
    _____
    _____

# 10 accomplishments I am proud of...

1. _____
   _____
   _____
   _____

2. _____
   _____
   _____
   _____

3. _____
   _____
   _____
   _____

4. _____
   _____
   _____
   _____

5. _____
   _____
   _____
   _____

6. _____
   _____
   _____
   _____

7. _____
   _____
   _____
   _____

Marla J. Albertie, M. Ed.

8. _____
   _____
   _____
   _____

9. _____
   _____
   _____
   _____

10. _____
    _____
    _____
    _____

# 25 reasons *I am freaking awesome...*

1. _____
   _____
   _____
   _____

2. _____
   _____
   _____
   _____

3. _____
   _____
   _____
   _____

4. _____
   _____
   _____
   _____

5. _____
   _____
   _____
   _____

6. _____
   _____
   _____
   _____

7. _____
   _____
   _____
   _____

Marla J. Albertie, M. Ed.

8. _____
   _____
   _____
   _____

9. _____
   _____
   _____
   _____

10. _____
    _____
    _____
    _____

11. _____
    _____
    _____
    _____

12. _____
    _____
    _____
    _____

13. _____
    _____
    _____
    _____

14. _____
    _____
    _____

15. _____
    _____
    _____
    _____

16. _____
_____
_____
_____

17. _____
_____
_____
_____

18. _____
_____
_____
_____

19. _____
_____
_____
_____

20. _____
_____
_____
_____

21. _____
_____
_____
_____

22. _____
_____
_____

23. _____
_____
_____
_____

24. _____
    _____
    _____
    _____

25. _____
    _____
    _____
    _____

# 25 values I live by...

1. _____
   _____
   _____
   _____

2. _____
   _____
   _____
   _____

3. _____
   _____
   _____
   _____

4. _____
   _____
   _____
   _____

5. _____
   _____
   _____

6. _____
   _____
   _____

7. _____
   _____
   _____

Marla J. Albertie, M. Ed.

8. _____
_____
_____
_____

9. _____
_____
_____
_____

10. _____
_____
_____
_____

11. _____
_____
_____
_____

12. _____
_____
_____
_____

13. _____
_____
_____
_____

14. _____
_____
_____
_____

15. _____
_____
_____
_____

16. _____
_____
_____
_____

17. _____
_____
_____
_____

18. _____
_____
_____
_____

19. _____
_____
_____
_____

20. _____
_____
_____
_____

21. _____
_____
_____
_____

22. _____
_____
_____

23. _____
_____
_____
_____

Marla J. Albertie, M. Ed.

24. _____
    _____
    _____
    _____

25. _____
    _____
    _____
    _____

## 20 things I am super great at...

1. _____
_____
_____
_____

2. _____
_____
_____
_____

3. _____
_____
_____
_____

4. _____
_____
_____
_____

5. _____
_____
_____
_____

6. _____
_____
_____
_____

7. _____
_____
_____
_____

Marla J. Albertie, M. Ed.

8. _____
_____
_____
_____

9. _____
_____
_____
_____

10. _____
_____
_____
_____

11. _____
_____
_____
_____

12. _____
_____
_____
_____

13. _____
_____
_____
_____

14. _____
_____
_____
_____

15. _____
_____
_____
_____

16. _____
_____
_____
_____

17. _____
_____
_____
_____

18. _____
_____
_____
_____

19. _____
_____
_____
_____

20. _____
_____
_____
_____

Marla J. Albertie, M. Ed.

# *I am a boss in these 10 areas...*

1. _____
   _____
   _____
   _____

2. _____
   _____
   _____
   _____

3. _____
   _____
   _____
   _____

4. _____
   _____
   _____
   _____

5. _____
   _____
   _____
   _____

6. _____
   _____
   _____
   _____

7. _____
   _____
   _____
   _____

8. _____
   _____
   _____
   _____

9. _____
   _____
   _____
   _____

10. _____
    _____
    _____
    _____

# 10 meals I can cook...

1. _____
   _____
   _____
   _____

2. _____
   _____
   _____
   _____

3. _____
   _____
   _____

4. _____
   _____
   _____

5. _____
   _____
   _____

6. _____
   _____
   _____

7. _____
   _____
   _____

8. _____
   _____
   _____
   _____

9. _____
   _____
   _____
   _____

10. _____
    _____
    _____
    _____

## 10 meals I want to learn to cook...

1. _____
   _____
   _____
   _____

2. _____
   _____
   _____
   _____

3. _____
   _____
   _____

4. _____
   _____
   _____

5. _____
   _____
   _____

6. _____
   _____
   _____

7. _____
   _____
   _____
   _____

8. _____
   _____
   _____
   _____

9. _____
   _____
   _____
   _____

10. _____
    _____
    _____
    _____

# 20 cities I have been to...

1. _____
   _____
   _____
   _____

2. _____
   _____
   _____
   _____

3. _____
   _____
   _____
   _____

4. _____
   _____
   _____
   _____

5. _____
   _____
   _____
   _____

6. _____
   _____
   _____
   _____

7. _____
   _____
   _____
   _____

8. _____
_____
_____
_____
_____

9. _____
_____
_____
_____

10. _____
_____
_____
_____

11. _____
_____
_____
_____

12. _____
_____
_____
_____

13. _____
_____
_____
_____

14. _____
_____
_____
_____

15. _____
_____
_____
_____

Marla J. Albertie, M. Ed.

16. _____
_____
_____
_____

17. _____
_____
_____
_____

18. _____
_____
_____
_____

19. _____
_____
_____
_____

20. _____
_____
_____
_____

# 25 cities *I* want to travel to...

1. _____
   _____
   _____
   _____

2. _____
   _____
   _____
   _____

3. _____
   _____
   _____
   _____

4. _____
   _____
   _____
   _____

5. _____
   _____
   _____
   _____

6. _____
   _____
   _____
   _____

7. _____
   _____
   _____
   _____

Marla J. Albertie, M. Ed.

8. _____
   _____
   _____
   _____

9. _____
   _____
   _____
   _____

10. _____
    _____
    _____
    _____

11. _____
    _____
    _____
    _____

12. _____
    _____
    _____
    _____

13. _____
    _____
    _____
    _____

14. _____
    _____
    _____

15. _____
    _____
    _____
    _____

16. _____

_____

_____

_____

17. _____

_____

_____

_____

18. _____

_____

_____

_____

19. _____

_____

_____

_____

20. _____

_____

_____

_____

21. _____

_____

_____

_____

22. _____

_____

_____

_____

23. _____

_____

_____

_____

24. _____

_____

_____

_____

25. _____

_____

_____

_____

# 10 strengths of mine are...

1. _____
   _____
   _____
   _____

2. _____
   _____
   _____
   _____

3. _____
   _____
   _____

4. _____
   _____
   _____
   _____

5. _____
   _____
   _____

6. _____
   _____
   _____

7. _____
   _____
   _____

Marla J. Albertie, M. Ed.

8. _____
   _____
   _____
   _____

9. _____
   _____
   _____
   _____

10. _____
    _____
    _____
    _____

*I have sexy ass_____: Fill in*
*the blank list as many as you want*

_____
_____
_____

_____
_____
_____

_____
_____
_____

_____
_____
_____

_____
_____
_____

_____
_____
_____

_____
_____
_____

Marla J. Albertie, M. Ed.

# 10 products you can't live without...

1. _____
   _____
   _____
   _____

2. _____
   _____
   _____
   _____

3. _____
   _____
   _____
   _____

4. _____
   _____
   _____
   _____

5. _____
   _____
   _____
   _____

6. _____
   _____
   _____

7. _____
   _____
   _____
   _____

Marla J. Albertie, M. Ed.

8. _____
   _____
   _____
   _____

9. _____
   _____
   _____
   _____

10. _____
    _____
    _____
    _____

# 10 quotes I made up...

1. _____
   _____
   _____
   _____

2. _____
   _____
   _____
   _____

3. _____
   _____
   _____
   _____

4. _____
   _____
   _____
   _____

5. _____
   _____
   _____
   _____

6. _____
   _____
   _____
   _____

7. _____
   _____
   _____
   _____

Marla J. Albertie, M. Ed.

8. _____
   _____
   _____
   _____

9. _____
   _____
   _____
   _____

10. _____
    _____
    _____
    _____

## 10 characteristics about myself that astound me...

1. _____
_____
_____
_____

2. _____
_____
_____
_____

3. _____
_____
_____
_____

4. _____
_____
_____
_____

5. _____
_____
_____

6. _____
_____
_____
_____

7. _____
_____
_____
_____

Marla J. Albertie, M. Ed.

8. _____
   _____
   _____
   _____

9. _____
   _____
   _____
   _____

10. _____
    _____
    _____
    _____

# 10 quotes I love...

1. _____
   _____
   _____
   _____

2. _____
   _____
   _____
   _____

3. _____
   _____
   _____
   _____

4. _____
   _____
   _____
   _____

5. _____
   _____
   _____
   _____

6. _____
   _____
   _____

7. _____
   _____
   _____
   _____

Marla J. Albertie, M. Ed.

8. _____
   _____
   _____
   _____

9. _____
   _____
   _____
   _____

10. _____
    _____
    _____
    _____

## 20 women *I* want to meet...

1. _____
   _____
   _____
   _____

2. _____
   _____
   _____
   _____

3. _____
   _____
   _____
   _____

4. _____
   _____
   _____
   _____

5. _____
   _____
   _____
   _____

6. _____
   _____
   _____
   _____

7. _____
   _____
   _____
   _____

Marla J. Albertie, M. Ed.

8. _____
   _____
   _____
   _____

9. _____
   _____
   _____
   _____

10. _____
    _____
    _____
    _____

# 10 companies I could run if I were the CEO...

1. _____
   _____
   _____
   _____

2. _____
   _____
   _____
   _____

3. _____
   _____
   _____
   _____

4. _____
   _____
   _____
   _____

5. _____
   _____
   _____
   _____

6. _____
   _____
   _____
   _____

7. _____
   _____
   _____
   _____

Marla J. Albertie, M. Ed.

8. _____
   _____
   _____
   _____

9. _____
   _____
   _____
   _____

10. _____
    _____
    _____
    _____

*15 words others would use to describe me...*

1. _____
   _____
   _____
   _____

2. _____
   _____
   _____
   _____

3. _____
   _____
   _____
   _____

4. _____
   _____
   _____
   _____

5. _____
   _____
   _____
   _____

6. _____
   _____
   _____

7. _____
   _____
   _____
   _____

8. _____
   _____
   _____
   _____
   _____

9. _____
   _____
   _____
   _____

10. _____
    _____
    _____
    _____

11. _____
    _____
    _____
    _____

12. _____
    _____
    _____
    _____

13. _____
    _____
    _____
    _____

14. _____
    _____
    _____
    _____

15. _____
    _____
    _____
    _____

# *10 things that make me smile...*

1. _____
   _____
   _____
   _____

2. _____
   _____
   _____
   _____

3. _____
   _____
   _____
   _____

4. _____
   _____
   _____
   _____

5. _____
   _____
   _____
   _____

6. _____
   _____
   _____
   _____

7. _____
   _____
   _____
   _____

Marla J. Albertie, M. Ed.

8. _____
_____
_____
_____

9. _____
_____
_____
_____

10. _____
_____
_____
_____

## 10 things that motivate me...

1. _____
   _____
   _____
   _____

2. _____
   _____
   _____
   _____

3. _____
   _____
   _____
   _____

4. _____
   _____
   _____
   _____

5. _____
   _____
   _____

6. _____
   _____
   _____

7. _____
   _____
   _____

Marla J. Albertie, M. Ed.

8. _____
_____
_____
_____

9. _____
_____
_____
_____

10. _____
_____
_____
_____

## 30 things I would do if money were not an issue...

1. _____
   _____
   _____
   _____

2. _____
   _____
   _____
   _____

3. _____
   _____
   _____
   _____

4. _____
   _____
   _____
   _____

5. _____
   _____
   _____
   _____

6. _____
   _____
   _____

7. _____
   _____
   _____
   _____

Marla J. Albertie, M. Ed.

8. _____
_____
_____
_____

9. _____
_____
_____
_____

10. _____
_____
_____
_____

11. _____
_____
_____
_____

12. _____
_____
_____
_____

13. _____
_____
_____
_____

14. _____
_____
_____

15. _____
_____
_____
_____

16. _____
_____
_____
_____

17. _____
_____
_____
_____

18. _____
_____
_____
_____

19. _____
_____
_____
_____

20. _____
_____
_____
_____

21. _____
_____
_____
_____

22. _____
_____
_____
_____

23. _____
_____
_____
_____

Marla J. Albertie, M. Ed.

24. _____
_____
_____
_____

25. _____
_____
_____
_____

26. _____
_____
_____
_____

27. _____
_____
_____
_____

28. _____
_____
_____
_____

29. _____
_____
_____
_____

30. _____
_____
_____
_____

# 10 beautiful things I own...

1. _____
   _____
   _____
   _____

2. _____
   _____
   _____
   _____

3. _____
   _____
   _____

4. _____
   _____
   _____

5. _____
   _____
   _____

6. _____
   _____
   _____

7. _____
   _____
   _____
   _____

Marla J. Albertie, M. Ed.

8. _____
_____
_____
_____

9. _____
_____
_____
_____

10. _____
_____
_____
_____

# 10 things of beauty I adore...

1. _____
   _____
   _____
   _____

2. _____
   _____
   _____
   _____

3. _____
   _____
   _____
   _____

4. _____
   _____
   _____
   _____

5. _____
   _____
   _____

6. _____
   _____
   _____
   _____

7. _____
   _____
   _____
   _____

Marla J. Albertie, M. Ed.

8. _____
   _____
   _____
   _____

9. _____
   _____
   _____
   _____

10. _____
    _____
    _____
    _____

# My 5 favorite flowers...

1. _____
   _____
   _____
   _____

2. _____
   _____
   _____
   _____

3. _____
   _____
   _____
   _____

4. _____
   _____
   _____
   _____

5. _____
   _____
   _____
   _____

Marla J. Albertie, M. Ed.

## 10 favorite foods I like...

1. _____
   _____
   _____
   _____

2. _____
   _____
   _____
   _____

3. _____
   _____
   _____
   _____

4. _____
   _____
   _____
   _____

5. _____
   _____
   _____
   _____

6. _____
   _____
   _____
   _____

7. _____
   _____
   _____
   _____

8. _____

   _____

   _____

   _____

9. _____

   _____

   _____

   _____

10. _____

   _____

   _____

   _____

Marla J. Albertie, M. Ed.

# My 10 favorite TV shows...

1. _____
   _____
   _____
   _____

2. _____
   _____
   _____
   _____

3. _____
   _____
   _____
   _____

4. _____
   _____
   _____
   _____

5. _____
   _____
   _____
   _____

6. _____
   _____
   _____
   _____

7. _____
   _____
   _____
   _____

8. _____

   _____

   _____

   _____

9. _____

   _____

   _____

   _____

10. _____

   _____

   _____

   _____

# My 20 favorite movies...

1. _____
   _____
   _____
   _____

2. _____
   _____
   _____
   _____

3. _____
   _____
   _____
   _____

4. _____
   _____
   _____
   _____

5. _____
   _____
   _____
   _____

6. _____
   _____
   _____
   _____

7. _____
   _____
   _____
   _____

8. _____
_____
_____
_____

9. _____
_____
_____
_____

10. _____
_____
_____
_____

11. _____
_____
_____
_____

12. _____
_____
_____
_____

13. _____
_____
_____
_____

14. _____
_____
_____
_____

15. _____
_____
_____
_____

Marla J. Albertie, M. Ed.

16. _____
    _____
    _____
    _____

17. _____
    _____
    _____
    _____

18. _____
    _____
    _____
    _____

19. _____
    _____
    _____
    _____

20. _____
    _____
    _____
    _____

# 10 of my closest friends...

1. _____
   _____
   _____
   _____

2. _____
   _____
   _____
   _____

3. _____
   _____
   _____
   _____

4. _____
   _____
   _____
   _____

5. _____
   _____
   _____
   _____

6. _____
   _____
   _____

7. _____
   _____
   _____

Marla J. Albertie, M. Ed.

8. _____
   _____
   _____
   _____

9. _____
   _____
   _____
   _____

10. _____
    _____
    _____
    _____

# My 10 favorite food trucks...

1. _____
   _____
   _____
   _____

2. _____
   _____
   _____
   _____

3. _____
   _____
   _____
   _____

4. _____
   _____
   _____
   _____

5. _____
   _____
   _____
   _____

6. _____
   _____
   _____
   _____

7. _____
   _____
   _____
   _____

Marla J. Albertie, M. Ed.

8. _____
   _____
   _____
   _____
   _____

9. _____
   _____
   _____
   _____
   _____

10. _____
    _____
    _____
    _____

# My 10 favorite restaurants...

1. _____
   _____
   _____
   _____

2. _____
   _____
   _____
   _____

3. _____
   _____
   _____
   _____

4. _____
   _____
   _____
   _____

5. _____
   _____
   _____
   _____

6. _____
   _____
   _____
   _____

7. _____
   _____
   _____
   _____

Marla J. Albertie, M. Ed.

8. _____
   _____
   _____
   _____

9. _____
   _____
   _____
   _____

10. _____
    _____
    _____
    _____

*10 simple things that bring me joy...*

1. _____
   _____
   _____
   _____

2. _____
   _____
   _____
   _____

3. _____
   _____
   _____
   _____

4. _____
   _____
   _____
   _____

5. _____
   _____
   _____
   _____

6. _____
   _____
   _____
   _____

7. _____
   _____
   _____
   _____

Marla J. Albertie, M. Ed.

8. _____
   _____
   _____
   _____

9. _____
   _____
   _____
   _____

10. _____
    _____
    _____
    _____

## 10 facts about me no one knows...

1. _____
   _____
   _____
   _____

2. _____
   _____
   _____
   _____

3. _____
   _____
   _____
   _____

4. _____
   _____
   _____
   _____

5. _____
   _____
   _____
   _____

6. _____
   _____
   _____

7. _____
   _____
   _____
   _____

Marla J. Albertie, M. Ed.

8. _____
   _____
   _____
   _____

9. _____
   _____
   _____
   _____

10. _____
    _____
    _____
    _____

## *10 charities I give to or volunteer...*

1. _____
   _____
   _____
   _____

2. _____
   _____
   _____
   _____

3. _____
   _____
   _____
   _____

4. _____
   _____
   _____
   _____

5. _____
   _____
   _____

6. _____
   _____
   _____
   _____

7. _____
   _____
   _____
   _____

Marla J. Albertie, M. Ed.

8. _____
   _____
   _____
   _____

9. _____
   _____
   _____
   _____

10. _____
    _____
    _____
    _____

# 5 names of charities I would start...

1. _____
   _____
   _____
   _____

2. _____
   _____
   _____
   _____

3. _____
   _____
   _____
   _____

4. _____
   _____
   _____
   _____

5. _____
   _____
   _____
   _____

Marla J. Albertie, M. Ed.

*5 types of businesses I would start...*

1. _____
   _____
   _____
   _____

2. _____
   _____
   _____
   _____

3. _____
   _____
   _____
   _____

4. _____
   _____
   _____

5. _____
   _____
   _____
   _____

# 10 blogs I love to read...

1. _____
   _____
   _____
   _____

2. _____
   _____
   _____
   _____

3. _____
   _____
   _____
   _____

4. _____
   _____
   _____
   _____

5. _____
   _____
   _____

6. _____
   _____
   _____
   _____

7. _____
   _____
   _____

Marla J. Albertie, M. Ed.

8. _____

_____

_____

_____

9. _____

_____

_____

_____

10. _____

_____

_____

_____

*5 charities I donate to...*

1. _____
   _____
   _____
   _____

2. _____
   _____
   _____
   _____

3. _____
   _____
   _____

4. _____
   _____
   _____
   _____

5. _____
   _____
   _____
   _____

Marla J. Albertie, M. Ed.

# 15 women *I would love to interview...*

1. _____
   _____
   _____
   _____

2. _____
   _____
   _____
   _____

3. _____
   _____
   _____
   _____

4. _____
   _____
   _____
   _____

5. _____
   _____
   _____

6. _____
   _____
   _____
   _____

7. _____
   _____
   _____
   _____

8. _____
   _____
   _____
   _____

9. _____
   _____
   _____
   _____

10. _____
    _____
    _____
    _____

11. _____
    _____
    _____
    _____

12. _____
    _____
    _____
    _____

13. _____
    _____
    _____
    _____

14. _____
    _____
    _____
    _____

15. _____
    _____
    _____
    _____

Marla J. Albertie, M. Ed.

# 10 furniture pieces I love...

1. _____
   _____
   _____
   _____

2. _____
   _____
   _____
   _____

3. _____
   _____
   _____
   _____

4. _____
   _____
   _____
   _____

5. _____
   _____
   _____
   _____

6. _____
   _____
   _____
   _____

7. _____
   _____
   _____
   _____

8. _____
   _____
   _____
   _____

9. _____
   _____
   _____
   _____

10. _____
    _____
    _____
    _____

# 10 podcasts I love...

1. _____
   _____
   _____
   _____

2. _____
   _____
   _____
   _____

3. _____
   _____
   _____
   _____

4. _____
   _____
   _____
   _____

5. _____
   _____
   _____
   _____

6. _____
   _____
   _____
   _____

7. _____
   _____
   _____
   _____

8. _____
   _____
   _____
   _____

9. _____
   _____
   _____
   _____

10. _____
    _____
    _____
    _____

## 20 books I love that are a must read for anyone...

1. _____
   _____
   _____
   _____

2. _____
   _____
   _____
   _____

3. _____
   _____
   _____
   _____

4. _____
   _____
   _____
   _____

5. _____
   _____
   _____
   _____

6. _____
   _____
   _____
   _____

7. _____
   _____
   _____
   _____

8. _____
   _____
   _____
   _____

9. _____
   _____
   _____
   _____

10. _____
    _____
    _____
    _____

11. _____
    _____
    _____
    _____

12. _____
    _____
    _____
    _____

13. _____
    _____
    _____
    _____

14. _____
    _____
    _____
    _____

15. _____
    _____
    _____
    _____

Marla J. Albertie, M. Ed.

16. _____

_____

_____

_____

17. _____

_____

_____

_____

18. _____

_____

_____

_____

19. _____

_____

_____

_____

20. _____

_____

_____

_____

# 15 stores I love...

1. _____
   _____
   _____
   _____

2. _____
   _____
   _____
   _____

3. _____
   _____
   _____
   _____

4. _____
   _____
   _____
   _____

5. _____
   _____
   _____
   _____

6. _____
   _____
   _____
   _____

7. _____
   _____
   _____
   _____

Marla J. Albertie, M. Ed.

8. _____
   _____
   _____
   _____

9. _____
   _____
   _____
   _____

10. _____
    _____
    _____
    _____

11. _____
    _____
    _____
    _____

12. _____
    _____
    _____
    _____

13. _____
    _____
    _____
    _____

14. _____
    _____
    _____

15. _____
    _____
    _____
    _____

# 10 things I would invent...

1. _____
_____
_____
_____

2. _____
_____
_____
_____

3. _____
_____
_____
_____

4. _____
_____
_____
_____

5. _____
_____
_____
_____

6. _____
_____
_____
_____

7. _____
_____
_____
_____

Marla J. Albertie, M. Ed.

8. _____
   _____
   _____
   _____

9. _____
   _____
   _____
   _____

10. _____
    _____
    _____
    _____

# My 20 favorite singers...

1. _____
   _____
   _____
   _____

2. _____
   _____
   _____
   _____

3. _____
   _____
   _____
   _____

4. _____
   _____
   _____
   _____

5. _____
   _____
   _____

6. _____
   _____
   _____

7. _____
   _____
   _____

Marla J. Albertie, M. Ed.

8. _____
   _____
   _____
   _____

9. _____
   _____
   _____
   _____

10. _____
    _____
    _____
    _____

11. _____
    _____
    _____
    _____

12. _____
    _____
    _____
    _____

13. _____
    _____
    _____
    _____

14. _____
    _____
    _____
    _____

15. _____
    _____
    _____
    _____

16. _____
_____
_____
_____
_____

17. _____
_____
_____
_____
_____

18. _____
_____
_____
_____
_____

19. _____
_____
_____
_____
_____

20. _____
_____
_____
_____
_____

Marla J. Albertie, M. Ed.

# 10 live concerts I have attended...

1. _____
   _____
   _____
   _____

2. _____
   _____
   _____
   _____

3. _____
   _____
   _____
   _____

4. _____
   _____
   _____
   _____

5. _____
   _____
   _____
   _____

6. _____
   _____
   _____
   _____

7. _____
   _____
   _____
   _____

8. _____
   _____
   _____
   _____

9. _____
   _____
   _____
   _____

10. _____
    _____
    _____
    _____

Marla J. Albertie, M. Ed.

## 10 of my favorite drinks...

1. _____
_____
_____
_____

2. _____
_____
_____
_____

3. _____
_____
_____

4. _____
_____
_____

5. _____
_____
_____

6. _____
_____
_____

7. _____
_____
_____
_____

8. _____
   _____
   _____
   _____

9. _____
   _____
   _____
   _____

10. _____
    _____
    _____
    _____

## 5 sports I like...

1. _____
   _____
   _____
   _____

2. _____
   _____
   _____
   _____

3. _____
   _____
   _____
   _____

4. _____
   _____
   _____

5. _____
   _____
   _____
   _____

# 10 fashion designers I like...

1. _____
   _____
   _____
   _____

2. _____
   _____
   _____
   _____

3. _____
   _____
   _____
   _____

4. _____
   _____
   _____
   _____

5. _____
   _____
   _____
   _____

6. _____
   _____
   _____
   _____

7. _____
   _____
   _____

Marla J. Albertie, M. Ed.

8. _____
   _____
   _____
   _____

9. _____
   _____
   _____
   _____

10. _____
    _____
    _____
    _____

## 20 qualities I want for a romantic relationship...

1. _____
   _____
   _____
   _____

2. _____
   _____
   _____
   _____

3. _____
   _____
   _____
   _____

4. _____
   _____
   _____
   _____

5. _____
   _____
   _____
   _____

6. _____
   _____
   _____
   _____

7. _____
   _____
   _____
   _____

Marla J. Albertie, M. Ed.

8. _____
   _____
   _____
   _____

9. _____
   _____
   _____
   _____

10. _____
    _____
    _____

11. _____
    _____
    _____
    _____

12. _____
    _____
    _____
    _____

13. _____
    _____
    _____
    _____

14. _____
    _____
    _____

15. _____
    _____
    _____
    _____

16. _____
_____
_____
_____

17. _____
_____
_____
_____

18. _____
_____
_____
_____

19. _____
_____
_____
_____

20. _____
_____
_____
_____

Marla J. Albertie, M. Ed.

*My top 10 tips for motherhood...*

1. _____
   _____
   _____
   _____
   _____

2. _____
   _____
   _____
   _____
   _____

3. _____
   _____
   _____
   _____

4. _____
   _____
   _____
   _____

5. _____
   _____
   _____
   _____

6. _____
   _____
   _____
   _____

7. _____
   _____
   _____
   _____

8. _____
   _____
   _____
   _____

9. _____
   _____
   _____
   _____

10. _____
    _____
    _____
    _____

# 10 things that must be listed in my obituary...

1. _____
   _____
   _____
   _____

2. _____
   _____
   _____
   _____

3. _____
   _____
   _____
   _____

4. _____
   _____
   _____
   _____

5. _____
   _____
   _____
   _____

6. _____
   _____
   _____
   _____

7. _____
   _____
   _____
   _____

8. _____
   _____
   _____
   _____

9. _____
   _____
   _____
   _____

10. _____
    _____
    _____
    _____

# 10 things I learned from my parents...

1. _____
   _____
   _____
   _____

2. _____
   _____
   _____
   _____

3. _____
   _____
   _____
   _____

4. _____
   _____
   _____
   _____

5. _____
   _____
   _____
   _____

6. _____
   _____
   _____
   _____

7. _____
   _____
   _____
   _____

8. _____
   _____
   _____
   _____

9. _____
   _____
   _____
   _____

10. _____
    _____
    _____
    _____

Marla J. Albertie, M. Ed.

## 10 side hustles I want to try...

1. _____
   _____
   _____
   _____

2. _____
   _____
   _____
   _____

3. _____
   _____
   _____
   _____

4. _____
   _____
   _____
   _____

5. _____
   _____
   _____
   _____

6. _____
   _____
   _____
   _____

7. _____
   _____
   _____
   _____

8. _____
   _____
   _____
   _____

9. _____
   _____
   _____
   _____

10. _____
    _____
    _____
    _____

## 10 reasons why a company should hire you...

1. _____
   _____
   _____
   _____

2. _____
   _____
   _____
   _____

3. _____
   _____
   _____
   _____

4. _____
   _____
   _____
   _____

5. _____
   _____
   _____
   _____

6. _____
   _____
   _____
   _____

7. _____
   _____
   _____
   _____

8. _____

   _____

   _____

   _____

9. _____

   _____

   _____

   _____

10. _____

    _____

    _____

    _____

## 10 jobs I have held...

1. _____
   _____
   _____
   _____

2. _____
   _____
   _____
   _____

3. _____
   _____
   _____
   _____

4. _____
   _____
   _____
   _____

5. _____
   _____
   _____
   _____

6. _____
   _____
   _____
   _____

7. _____
   _____
   _____
   _____

8. _____

   _____

   _____

   _____

9. _____

   _____

   _____

   _____

10. _____

    _____

    _____

    _____

# 20 skills I have...

1. _____
_____
_____
_____

2. _____
_____
_____
_____

3. _____
_____
_____
_____

4. _____
_____
_____
_____

5. _____
_____
_____
_____

6. _____
_____
_____
_____

7. _____
_____
_____
_____

8. _____
_____
_____
_____

9. _____
_____
_____
_____

10. _____
_____
_____
_____

11. _____
_____
_____
_____

12. _____
_____
_____
_____

13. _____
_____
_____
_____

14. _____
_____
_____
_____

15. _____
_____
_____
_____

Marla J. Albertie, M. Ed.

16. _____
_____
_____
_____

17. _____
_____
_____
_____

18. _____
_____
_____
_____

19. _____
_____
_____
_____

20. _____
_____
_____
_____

## 10 things I would tell your 16-21 year-old self...

1. _____
   _____
   _____
   _____

2. _____
   _____
   _____
   _____

3. _____
   _____
   _____
   _____

4. _____
   _____
   _____
   _____

5. _____
   _____
   _____
   _____

6. _____
   _____
   _____
   _____

7. _____
   _____
   _____
   _____

Marla J. Albertie, M. Ed.

8. _____
   _____
   _____
   _____

9. _____
   _____
   _____
   _____

10. _____
    _____
    _____
    _____

# 10 things that are my guilty pleasures...

1. _____
   _____
   _____
   _____

2. _____
   _____
   _____
   _____

3. _____
   _____
   _____
   _____

4. _____
   _____
   _____
   _____

5. _____
   _____
   _____
   _____

6. _____
   _____
   _____
   _____

7. _____
   _____
   _____
   _____

Marla J. Albertie, M. Ed.

8. _____
   _____
   _____
   _____

9. _____
   _____
   _____
   _____

10. _____
   _____
   _____
   _____

# My 5 favorite subjects...

1. _____
   _____
   _____
   _____

2. _____
   _____
   _____
   _____

3. _____
   _____
   _____
   _____

4. _____
   _____
   _____

5. _____
   _____
   _____
   _____

Marla J. Albertie, M. Ed.

## My 2 favorite airlines...

1. _____
   _____
   _____
   _____

2. _____
   _____
   _____
   _____

# My 5 favorite artists...

1. _____
   _____
   _____
   _____

2. _____
   _____
   _____
   _____

3. _____
   _____
   _____
   _____

4. _____
   _____
   _____

5. _____
   _____
   _____
   _____

Marla J. Albertie, M. Ed.

# My 5 favorite hairstyles...

1. _____
_____
_____
_____

2. _____
_____
_____
_____

3. _____
_____
_____
_____

4. _____
_____
_____

5. _____
_____
_____
_____

## 3 award shows I must watch...

1. _____
   _____
   _____
   _____

2. _____
   _____
   _____
   _____

3. _____
   _____
   _____
   _____

# My 10 favorite games to play...

1. _____
   _____
   _____
   _____

2. _____
   _____
   _____
   _____

3. _____
   _____
   _____

4. _____
   _____
   _____
   _____

5. _____
   _____
   _____

6. _____
   _____
   _____

7. _____
   _____
   _____
   _____

8. _____
   _____
   _____
   _____

9. _____
   _____
   _____
   _____

10. _____
    _____
    _____
    _____

# 7 colors I like...

1. _____
   _____
   _____
   _____

2. _____
   _____
   _____
   _____

3. _____
   _____
   _____
   _____

4. _____
   _____
   _____

5. _____
   _____
   _____
   _____

6. _____
   _____
   _____
   _____

7. _____
   _____
   _____

*5 articles of clothing I like...*

1. _____
   _____
   _____
   _____

2. _____
   _____
   _____
   _____

3. _____
   _____
   _____
   _____

4. _____
   _____
   _____
   _____

5. _____
   _____
   _____
   _____

Marla J. Albertie, M. Ed.

## 2 instruments I want to learn to play...

1. _____
   _____
   _____
   _____

2. _____
   _____
   _____
   _____

*1 instrument I can play...*

1. _____
   _____
   _____
   _____

Marla J. Albertie, M. Ed.

# 5 magazines I must read...

1. _____
   _____
   _____
   _____

2. _____
   _____
   _____
   _____

3. _____
   _____
   _____
   _____

4. _____
   _____
   _____
   _____

5. _____
   _____
   _____
   _____

# 5 books I am thinking about writing...

1. _____
   _____
   _____
   _____

2. _____
   _____
   _____
   _____

3. _____
   _____
   _____
   _____

4. _____
   _____
   _____
   _____

5. _____
   _____
   _____
   _____

Marla J. Albertie, M. Ed.

# 6 laws I would pass...

1. _____
   _____
   _____
   _____

2. _____
   _____
   _____
   _____

3. _____
   _____
   _____
   _____

4. _____
   _____
   _____
   _____

5. _____
   _____
   _____
   _____

6. _____
   _____
   _____
   _____

*My favorite* _____ *rooms in the house are? Fill in the number*

_____
_____
_____
_____
_____
_____
_____
_____
_____
_____
_____
_____
_____
_____
_____
_____
_____
_____
_____
_____
_____
_____

# My 5 favorite alcoholic drinks...

1. _____
   _____
   _____
   _____

2. _____
   _____
   _____
   _____

3. _____
   _____
   _____

4. _____
   _____
   _____

5. _____
   _____
   _____
   _____

Marla J. Albertie, M. Ed.

# My 5 non-alcoholic drinks...

1. _____
   _____
   _____
   _____

2. _____
   _____
   _____
   _____

3. _____
   _____
   _____
   _____

4. _____
   _____
   _____

5. _____
   _____
   _____
   _____

# My 10 favorite people...

1. _____
   _____
   _____
   _____

2. _____
   _____
   _____
   _____

3. _____
   _____
   _____
   _____

4. _____
   _____
   _____
   _____

5. _____
   _____
   _____

6. _____
   _____
   _____

7. _____
   _____
   _____
   _____

Marla J. Albertie, M. Ed.

8. _____
_____
_____
_____

9. _____
_____
_____
_____

10. _____
_____
_____
_____

# My top 5 heroes...

1. _____
_____
_____
_____

2. _____
_____
_____
_____

3. _____
_____
_____
_____

4. _____
_____
_____
_____

5. _____
_____
_____
_____

Marla J. Albertie, M. Ed.

## 10 things that define your independence...

1. _____
   _____
   _____
   _____

2. _____
   _____
   _____
   _____

3. _____
   _____
   _____

4. _____
   _____
   _____

5. _____
   _____
   _____

6. _____
   _____
   _____

7. _____
   _____
   _____
   _____

8. _____
   _____
   _____
   _____

9. _____
   _____
   _____
   _____

10. _____
    _____
    _____
    _____

# Top 10 names of cities I created...

1. _____
   _____
   _____
   _____

2. _____
   _____
   _____
   _____

3. _____
   _____
   _____

4. _____
   _____
   _____

5. _____
   _____
   _____

6. _____
   _____
   _____

7. _____
   _____
   _____

8. _____

_____

_____

_____

9. _____

_____

_____

_____

10. _____

_____

_____

_____

Marla J. Albertie, M. Ed.

# 15 things I am itching to do...

1. _____
_____
_____
_____

2. _____
_____
_____
_____

3. _____
_____
_____
_____

4. _____
_____
_____
_____

5. _____
_____
_____
_____

6. _____
_____
_____
_____

7. _____
_____
_____
_____

8. _____

_____

_____

_____

9. _____

_____

_____

_____

10. _____

_____

_____

_____

11. _____

_____

_____

_____

12. _____

_____

_____

_____

13. _____

_____

_____

_____

14. _____

_____

_____

_____

15. _____

_____

_____

_____

## *10 things that turn me on...*

1. _____

   _____

   _____

   _____

2. _____

   _____

   _____

   _____

3. _____

   _____

   _____

4. _____

   _____

   _____

5. _____

   _____

   _____

6. _____

   _____

   _____

7. _____

   _____

   _____

   _____

8. _____

_____

_____

_____

_____

9. _____

_____

_____

_____

10. _____

_____

_____

_____

# My 15 favorite memories...

1. _____
   _____
   _____
   _____

2. _____
   _____
   _____
   _____

3. _____
   _____
   _____
   _____

4. _____
   _____
   _____

5. _____
   _____
   _____

6. _____
   _____
   _____

7. _____
   _____
   _____
   _____

8. _____
_____
_____
_____

9. _____
_____
_____
_____

10. _____
_____
_____
_____

11. _____
_____
_____
_____

12. _____
_____
_____
_____

13. _____
_____
_____
_____

14. _____
_____
_____
_____

15. _____
_____
_____
_____

# 10 truths about my astrological sign...

1. _____
   _____
   _____
   _____

2. _____
   _____
   _____
   _____

3. _____
   _____
   _____
   _____

4. _____
   _____
   _____
   _____

5. _____
   _____
   _____
   _____

6. _____
   _____
   _____
   _____

7. _____
   _____
   _____
   _____

8. _____
   _____
   _____
   _____

9. _____
   _____
   _____
   _____

10. _____
    _____
    _____
    _____

# My top 10 house rules...

1. _____
   _____
   _____
   _____

2. _____
   _____
   _____
   _____

3. _____
   _____
   _____

4. _____
   _____
   _____

5. _____
   _____
   _____

6. _____
   _____
   _____

7. _____
   _____
   _____

8. _____
   _____
   _____
   _____

9. _____
   _____
   _____
   _____

10. _____
    _____
    _____
    _____

# My 10 favorite fashion rules...

1. _____
   _____
   _____
   _____

2. _____
   _____
   _____
   _____

3. _____
   _____
   _____
   _____

4. _____
   _____
   _____
   _____

5. _____
   _____
   _____

6. _____
   _____
   _____

7. _____
   _____
   _____
   _____

8. _____
   _____
   _____
   _____

9. _____
   _____
   _____
   _____

10. _____
    _____
    _____
    _____

# 10 things I am obsessed with...

1. _____
   _____
   _____
   _____

2. _____
   _____
   _____
   _____

3. _____
   _____
   _____
   _____

4. _____
   _____
   _____
   _____

5. _____
   _____
   _____
   _____

6. _____
   _____
   _____
   _____

7. _____
   _____
   _____
   _____

8. _____
   _____
   _____
   _____
   _____

9. _____
   _____
   _____
   _____

10. _____
   _____
   _____
   _____

Marla J. Albertie, M. Ed.

## 10 things I want today but can't have but I will get one day!

1. _____
_____
_____
_____

2. _____
_____
_____
_____

3. _____
_____
_____
_____

4. _____
_____
_____
_____

5. _____
_____
_____
_____

6. _____
_____
_____
_____

7. _____
_____
_____
_____

8. _____

   _____

   _____

   _____

9. _____

   _____

   _____

   _____

10. _____

   _____

   _____

   _____

## My 5 favorite types of purses/bags...

1. _____

_____

_____

_____

2. _____

_____

_____

_____

3. _____

_____

_____

_____

4. _____

_____

_____

_____

5. _____

_____

_____

_____

# My 10 favorite Apps...

1. _____
   _____
   _____
   _____

2. _____
   _____
   _____
   _____

3. _____
   _____
   _____
   _____

4. _____
   _____
   _____
   _____

5. _____
   _____
   _____

6. _____
   _____
   _____

7. _____
   _____
   _____

Marla J. Albertie, M. Ed.

8. _____
   _____
   _____
   _____

9. _____
   _____
   _____
   _____

10. _____
    _____
    _____
    _____

# My 10 favorite casino games...

1. _____
   _____
   _____
   _____

2. _____
   _____
   _____
   _____

3. _____
   _____
   _____
   _____

4. _____
   _____
   _____
   _____

5. _____
   _____
   _____
   _____

6. _____
   _____
   _____
   _____

7. _____
   _____
   _____
   _____

Marla J. Albertie, M. Ed.

8. _____

   _____

   _____

   _____

9. _____

   _____

   _____

   _____

10. _____

   _____

   _____

   _____

*Now it is time for you to name some I may have missed. Use the next 10 pages to create your own...*

_____

_____

_____

_____

_____

_____

_____

_____

_____

_____

_____

_____

_____

_____

_____

_____

_____

_____

_____

_____

Marla J. Albertie, M. Ed.

Marla J. Albertie, M. Ed.

Marla J. Albertie, M. Ed.

Marla J. Albertie, M. Ed.

Marla J. Albertie, M. Ed.

# Epilogue

What did you discover about yourself?

I hope you enjoyed bragging about yourself as much as I enjoyed thinking of the questions. I love books and believe they should be for reading as well as having fun. I LOVE creating workbooks for people to love on themselves.

**Giving yourself the love you deserve is the best gift you can give yourself.**

If you want more information on loving yourself and creating harmony check out my website

www.truthspeakscoaching.com

Be sure to follow me:

Twitter: @tspeakscoaching

Medium: Truth Speaks Group or Marla J. Albertie

Instagram: tspeaksgroup

YouTube: Truth Speaks Group

Thank you!

www.ingramcontent.com/pod-product-compliance
Lightning Source LLC
Chambersburg PA
CBHW060510130626
46553CB00002B/446